ALSO BY
DARRYL S. DOANE and ROSE D. SLOAT

Life's Journey - Find Your Place to Stand and Build the Right Future©

Life's Journey - Find Your Place to Stand and Build the Right Future© Personal Journal

The Constant Customer - Keep them coming back again and again and again©

Excuses, Excuses, Excuses - For Not Delivering Excellent Customer Service and What Should Happen©

The Customer Service Activity©

50 Activities for Achieving Excellent Customer Service©

Stories They Will Remember©

The New Sales Game© Facilitator's Guide

The New Sales Game© Participant Manual

The Tiger & The Ringmaster

DARRYL S. DOANE and ROSE D. SLOAT

©2015, Darryl S. Doane and Rose D. Sloat

Dedication

We dedicate *The Tiger & The Ringmaster* to the NEO (Northeast Ohio) Givers for their inspiration and friendship and to all those who care enough to balance High Technology with High Touch (The Human Factor).

The Tiger & The Ringmaster

Foreword

How has high tech affected your career path?

Too direct of a question? Perhaps, like watching a solar eclipse, we must use a proxy. In the same manner, but what if one were to use a Bengal tiger cub and its growth to adulthood, to safely explore the question of how tech has, is, and will continue to shape our careers and our life's journey.

One bright August Friday afternoon in 2011, in walked Darryl and Rose. We three shared a common colleague, Greg Loo. It was at the launch of a new sort of networking group that Greg founded based on the tenets of a book, *The Go-Giver*, we four (and a few more), began an adventure that in more ways than one led to the creation of this book. Just as iron sharpens iron, one idea led to another, and a new magazine was born. Offering up my experience launching a print periodical some years earlier, together we created a framework that would assist in creating digital content for the Apple iPad and iPhone, Android phones and tablets, Kindle Fire and Nook HD "smart/mobile" platforms.

For fifteen months, month in and month out, week in and week out, I have watched Darryl and Rose (as publishers) curate the most amazing content for the digital magazine called **Life's Journey**, which began its life at that Friday afternoon networking event. They have contributed content as well and the very first issue included the first chapter of **The Tiger & The Ringmaster**, which is now complete and in your hands.

Time flies!

Find that comfortable spot and settle in for a great read... one that might just entertain and yet give pause at the same time. For me, the burning question became, how far down that rabbit hole of technology have we traveled?

Jeff 'SKI' Kinsey
Author, ***Purple Curve Effect***
August 2015

Introduction To The Tiger & The Ringmaster

Beware! The future is upon us.

This was the time of man, the time of machines, the time of high technology, and the time of High Touch or the Human Factor. But mankind in all its infinite knowledge had allowed its ego to get in the way, grown lazy, and uninvolved with the daily necessities of life. All was being left to the technology under the guise of "serving the best interests of mankind." This is a fable that is all too close to a direction we may be heading in faster than the speed of life. There may not be an opportunity to turn things around once we allow technology to devour our souls. This is a warning to move forward cautiously and respectfully of what we as humans not only have the ability to do but the choice to make decisions that will impact our very existence, and choices that will chart the course of our future and be moving us toward an unimaginable dark destiny. Our decisions and our actions may produce consequences for which we will be inescapably accountable.

This is a call to awareness. This is a warning of what may lie ahead should we choose to move from the mind of man blindly into the hands of technology just because we can! Weigh the possibilities, take practical risks, move forward with confidence and the knowledge that our decisions have been the result of thorough investigation and debate. Chart a cautious and predictable course of prosperity that utilizes the tools of technology in a beneficial and caring way for us all. The Human Factor is and must remain the primary component that is the key to a purposeful future.

Beware! The future is upon us.

Darryl S . Doane, Rose D. Sloat

Author Insights

Episode 1 - Introduction To Characters

There are a number of significant players in this story, and we would like to introduce you to them now. First and most significant is the central character to our story Hité. Hité is short for High Tech or High Technology. Hité is a Bengal tiger cub. His journey from a Bengal tiger cub to growth and development as a mature tiger is central to our story.

Another primary character is Teché, Hités father whose name is short for Technology. He is reflective of all that has transpired and evolved up to the birth of his new son and heir, Hité. And then, of course, there is Revoé, Hité's mother whose name is short for Revolution. She represents change, growth, development, newness, and energy and the transitioning of all that she has been to her newborn. The Ringmaster represents all of mankind, our humanity, our human consciousness and awareness, which must be on constant vigilance to protect the delicate balance that must coexist between High Tech and High Touch or Technology and the Human Factor.

The People's Popular Circus represents our world and the general population and the people living in it. Some minor players will be introduced throughout the story as it develops and their significance revealed as the story unfolds. Oh, and there is one more primary player that emerges near the conclusion of our tale and that is Innové, the new baby gazelle representing innovation and constant change.

Episode 1 – Introduction

We live in an incredible era. We have often been told that the one thing in life that we know is a certainty, that we can count on happening, and that we should expect is change itself. In this era change is occurring at a magnitude we have never experienced and never even anticipated. Modern technology is coming at us like a tidal wave. If we stand still, we will be swept away. The accumulated information on this planet is said to be doubling in size every three to four years and the technology approximately every fourteen to sixteen months. If not handled and dealt with properly, this active volcano may explode and do unimaginable damage in this fast-paced 21st century. And yet, it is a remarkable innovation that can lead us, if properly handled, on an incredibly successful journey.

The critical factor to properly handling this High Tech phenomenon is us, the people, each one of us—you are that critical factor in this equation. Each one of us needs to have the ability to build bridges of trust and credibility linking High Tech with High Touch—the Human Factor. Only then can we move forward with confidence to utilize the tools, the innovations, the skills and changes making up this new technology in the most appropriate and meaningful manner. Those bridges we build will allow us to deliver the service we intended to deliver in the first place. The Human Factor, people dealing with people, and the impact that has on the selection, use, and evolution of technology is what this book is about.

The birth of Hité, the Bengal tiger cub, was a well planned and much anticipated event. His father, Teché and his mother, Revoé had been carefully selected to produce the wonderful tiger cub they were so pleased with. The People's Popular Circus was the world in which they lived, it was their home and it was also the home of the Ringmaster.

Along with this birth came great expectations.

Truly a magnificent creature, Hité quickly became endeared to all who came into contact with him. This included not only the Ringmaster but all of the workers, their families and all those who occupied the People's Popular Circus. Hité quickly became commercialized and utilized by the People's Popular Circus. He became the center of attention and the main attraction to one and all. The marketing and promotions surrounding Hité mesmerized everyone. He was the latest trend and the greatest attraction and everyone wanted to possess and feel ownership of all that Hité was, even though, for the most part, they did not completely comprehend all that was before them and all that it truly encompassed.

The tiger cub grew rapidly. He seemed to double and triple in size and strength almost overnight. All were in awe over Hité's rapid acceleration and the power he demonstrated. His power seemed to grow in leaps and bounds every single day. And his ability to influence the entire environment of the People's Popular Circus was unparalleled. When individuals stood before Hité, they appeared to be totally engulfed in him to the total exclusion of what was going on around them with the other members of the People's Popular Circus. Oh, they communicated about, around, and through the activities of Hité, but they seemed to lose a sense of contact and intimacy with each other. Their focus had changed. Their sense of urgency had been realigned. Everything rotated around Hité who had become the center of their existence.

The Ringmaster was a caring, concerned individual and he represented the best interests of all the members of the People's Popular Circus. The Ringmaster educated and guided each member on how to best utilize Hité, their new star attraction. He reminded them that their actions should be purposeful and required the appropriate thought and consideration. The Ringmaster wanted to ensure that as Hité grew with the proper training, usage, and application, he would become an increasingly valuable asset and tool for the People's Popular Circus and serve their purpose well.
The Ringmaster knew that Hité must be tamed and his behavior and actions controlled and directed to ensure that his connection with the members of the People's Popular Circus and all the visitors they received would be beneficial. The Ringmaster also knew that Hité was like an active volcano with tremendous power and energy, which if not properly focused, tamed, understood, and responsively channeled, could potentially become an endangerment to those exposed to him and possibly a destructive force even unto Hité himself.

Episode 2 – Hité's Journey Continues

The birth of Hité had been so anticipated that people actually stood in line or often paid others to stand in line for them so that they would be able to be the first to see the new cub. They had anticipated his coming for so long, and now that Hité was here, they seemed incapable of satisfying their curiosity. The members of the People's Popular Circus gathered around, gazing at Hité in awe. His movements, color, sounds, and all that he was capable of was a marvel to behold.

Hité had little time to rest. He was always on stage. He was always performing and demonstrating his capabilities. The People's Popular Circus simply could not get enough of him and that resulted in an almost constant surveillance and scrutinizing of Hité's every movement. With every new skill he learned, Hité was applauded and encouraged to hurry up and master the next one.

From the moment Hité was born he was tracked. He had had chips implanted to provide analytics. The Ringmaster allowed this to take place. Ringmaster believed that this would allow Hité's Caretakers to know and understand Hité's capabilities and performance on a consistent basis. The Caretakers, however, were also expected to have the same chip used on them to provide information on their work. Some resented having their every move and whereabouts known. Some of the Caretakers gave it little thought but some felt a deep seated anger over this invasion of privacy. One of them in particular, Mr. Dee Leet, was furious over receiving the same treatment as Hité. It was very difficult for this particular Caretaker to live with this mandate given him.

Other happenings were beginning to occur that impacted many others within the People's Popular Circus. Some gathered in a coordinated effort to demonstrate the love they felt for Hité. They expressed how they cherished him and all the good things that he brought to the People's Popular Circus. However, there were also those who protested that Hité was replacing and taking away the necessary focus on other more critical items. There was too much time and effort being devoted to Hité that led to an overall neglect of significant things. Those enthralled with Hité were neglecting their families and friends. People did not communicate with the same attention as they had in the past.

This breakdown of effective listening skills prompted concern and even anger in some. They felt that one of the greatest courtesies one can extend to another person, listening and concentrating on another person with complete attention, was lost. This joy in life was being abandoned by many in the People's Popular Circus and it created concern. These so-called flash mobs were gathering on a regular basis (both the supportive and the critical ones) throughout Hité's early years of development.

Hité could not understand these happenings. He responded favorably to the positive attention and the almost borderline adoration, but he was confused when it came to the shouting and the name calling. There were even extreme demonstrations when items were thrown at Hité. On one occasion the cub was even poked with a stick.

Ringmaster watched and observed these actions with great caution and concern. He knew that the manner in which Hité was dealt with would have serious consequences on the People's Popular Circus. Properly directed and nurtured with care, Hité would have so much to offer. But with mistreatment and improper direction there was cause for great concern and the circus would soon begin to feel that impact in their world.

"In the past, those who foolishly sought power by riding on the back of the tiger ended up inside."
- John F. Kennedy
35th President of the United States

Author Insights

Episode 3 – Hité's World

In Episode 2 we talked about the Caretakers for the first time who have the primary responsibility of working with, caring for, and seeing that Hité is properly maintained and functional. They closely follow the instructions given to them by Ringmaster. Hité has a very complex schedule and the Caretakers are to make certain that all is properly implemented. Their responsibility is extremely important and requires a tremendous effort on their part. One of the Caretakers is Mr. Dee Leet, and he performs his duties well but resents some of the personal intrusions such as a tracking device and constant analytics that are not only implanted in Hité but in the Caretakers as well.

In Episode 3 we delve into Hité's world and introduce you to the Big Top and the various tents that exist under it. The Big Top is the environment under which all the Tents exist. Some of the major tents include the Ringtone Tent. Ringmaster resides here, and it is also the main operating base for Hité. The Ringtones have been the primary leaders under the Big Top and their influence is felt by all the other Tents. Their creativity has been the key differentiating factor that makes them stand out.

The Producers is the name given to another one of the primary Tents. The Caretakers reside here and as a result of that, they have a heightened awareness of all that is taking place under the Big Top. Remember, they accompany Hité everywhere he roams. That enables them to observe and gather a great deal of valuable information. The other Tent making up the Big 3 is the Futurist Tent. They concentrate on the accumulation of knowledge and believe that knowledge is the primary tool for shaping the direction those under the Big Top will move in. Creativity, Information, Knowledge—three essential ingredients for successfully moving forward and existing under the Big Top yet each of these 3 critical items was protected and guarded as a personal treasure by the Ringtones, the Producers, and the Futurists.

Episode 3 - Hité's World

Hité's world was extensive. The Big Top contained all the various Tents, where all members of the People's Popular Circus lived. These Tents were very individualistic and had their own identity. Each Tent's members took great pride in their lifestyles. For generations, one was expected to do what one's family had been in the past. This had gone on for as long as people could remember. It was the way things were done. Each Tent had a culture of its own, which over the years had created barriers in communication and at times even distrust with the other Tents. There were many other Tents in Hité's world, but they often tended to exist as worlds unto themselves. This lack of awareness and concern for each other created a disturbance in the balance that had existed in the past and promoted harmony. Each of the Tents did desire to exist in peace and prosperity but often their ambitions created obstacles.

Ringmaster was from the Ringtone Tent where Hité was born and this was his home base. The majority of the creative ideas that had driven the People's Popular Circus for the past fifty years had come from the Ringtone Tent. Under Ringmaster, the Ringtone Tent had flourished and prospered. The Ringtones, they called themselves, had influenced the ideas throughout the Big Top.

Ringmaster's leadership had been a driving force for not only the Ringtone Tent but for others under the Big Top. Ringmaster had been the primary individual who had set the course and charted the direction the People's Popular Circus moved in. Now, he was looking a bit thin and moving a little slower, and there was a growing concern about his general health. This created uneasiness, particularly within the Ringtone Tent.

In the middle of the People's Popular Circus was the Producers Tent. This was where the Caretakers lived along with many who made the majority of the items created by the Ringtones. As a result of their direct involvement with Hité, the Producers had grown in power and prestige.

The Ringtones tended to concentrate on the creation of ideas that would assist in making life more comfortable and promote a more relaxing flow and processing of events. The Producers on the other hand concentrated on taking those ideas and making them become a reality. In order to accomplish this they concentrated on effective communication, observing, and listening skills. In fact, recently there had become a larger number of individuals in the Producers Tent communicating effectively at all levels than in the Ringtone Tent. It was affecting the balance in the community.

Another dominant Tent under the Big Top was called the Futurists. They focused on the accumulation of knowledge and what was to be done. They were working on procedures identified by the other key Tents as essential to success. This knowledge base outstripped the other Tents. The Futurists wanted their piece of the pie and had a visionary plan to achieve that end.

All of the Tents often didn't realize how very much they needed each other's talents to achieve all that they desired in their world under the Big Top. However, things change. With the birth of Hité there seemed to be a growing focus on the tenacious pursuit of altered dreams. There was more focus on the enjoyment on that rather than on the roles and duties that had been performed in the past.

Hité was a critical component that had the capability to bring them together or to disrupt the natural flow of things. An even more critical component was every single individual that made up the People's Popular Circus – the Human Factor. This was the true tie that bound together everything under the Big Top and should be the deciding factor in what would benefit their world. However, many often abandoned that responsibility as they concentrated their attention on Hité.

The tradition of remaining in the same role and performing the same duties repeatedly was disappearing. Power was shifting around in new ways in the People's Popular Circus as Hité grew.

Hité's analytics and tracking systems doubled the information capabilities as he was allowed to roam with his Caretakers throughout the Big Top. The new information superseded much of the accumulated knowledge gathered even as recently as one year ago. As Hité grew, the record of his development grew. Everyone was challenged to remain current in their knowledge. Some began to realize - particularly those in the Futurist Tent - that what they had studied only two and three years before was now obsolete. Some began to feel that the information and capabilities that Hité possessed might eventually represent more than that contained in the sum total of the capabilities of all the inhabitants of the People's Popular Circus. This concerned many, including Ringmaster. No one wanted things to get out of control.

Episode 4 - Tiger Technology

Hité was the very embodiment of High Tech within the People's Popular Circus.

Ringmaster and the Caretakers measured Hité's development. They monitored his powerful muscles and massive build. Bengal tigers are beautiful animals. Hité's sleek coat, striped with his unique pattern, was researched. His eyes, perfectly adapted for night hunting, were tested in delicate experiments. His teeth and formidable jaw could efficiently handle anything – the Caretakers knew exactly how much. His parents had bequeathed him with extraordinary magnificence. Many members of the Circus thought he was the greatest tiger ever.

Hité had grown to nearly seven feet in length with a shoulder height of thirty-eight inches. Hité was smart. He learned tricks and tasks far faster than his parents Teché and Revoé had. Everyone agreed he was a superior specimen of Bengal tiger and was still not yet fully mature. The biggest question was whether he could be used to benefit the Circus, or to harm it.

People from each Tent asked each other what else would Hité be able to do? Speculation led to suggestions which in turn led to further technology to track the tiger's development.

Technology has the uncanny ability to mask a great deal of reality from people. Losing track of what was truly important happened slowly. Were the people of the Circus more interested in the technology than the tiger? In their fascination with Hité, some who may have cared about the tiger were distracted by the technology he embodied.

"Where is this going? What will it do to our world?" thought Ringmaster.

Ringmaster loved the People's Popular Circus - each Tent under the Big Top, every single individual. He did everything he could to protect their happiness and success. Hité's strength and influence were growing daily. Was the tiger a threat or a boon to the Circus? They had to find techniques to manage him in the best way. Information advanced the Circus's culture; the potential impact hadn't been considered. Changes, while necessary, would not come without cost.

Ringmaster heard one of the trainers say, "I can't wait until things begin to slow down."

Ringmaster knew it was highly unlikely for things to slow down. Technology was slipping away from the control of the people. What else would be swept away by this onslaught of innovation? The bridges of trust and credibility that Ringmaster had worked so hard to build between the Tents under the Big Top were being undermined with the influx of technology. It was simply too much, too fast, like an avalanche of data that would overtake those not moving fast enough.

What was happening to the old values? Focus on Hité had changed the Circus people. Were Ringmaster's efforts to educate the people enough to cope with the still immature Hité? Even Hité's roaming capabilities were more extensive than originally expected. No one was untouched by the tiger's influence.

No one completely understood why trust between the Tents started to fail. Hité brought feast and famine at the same time. He roamed throughout the People's Popular Circus, which provided information and awareness everywhere under the Big Top. That created a guarded concern in some. Ringmaster remembered a discovery of valuable metals had once hurt the People's Popular Circus. Greed, hostilities, and dissention had harmed the Circus community. He didn't want to repeat that.

What they needed to understand was that the people themselves had to retain their humanity as they became more interdependently involved with Hité. Who held their future? Hité or themselves?

All the elements under the Big Top must be taken into consideration while the Circus people determined how to manage this situation. They needed to establish a united sense of direction to keep Hité's world and the People's Popular Circus in sync with one another rather than on a collision course. High Tech and High Touch should thrive together where each of the Tents would peacefully and purposefully coexist.

Ringmaster began to plan.

Episode 5 – Touching Technology

Ringmaster knew that all the elements under the Big Top must be considered to determine a course of action. A unified direction would keep Hité's world and the People's Popular Circus in touch with one another. But how? The technical aspects of maintaining Hité and learning from him already caused rifts between the Tents. Resentment heightened between those who loved Hité and those who feared his influence on the People's Popular Circus.

Ringmaster periodically joined the Caretakers when they walked with the tiger around the Circus. Hité had been trained to let even the smallest children come near him safely. Ringmaster watched the people interact with the animal and with the Caretakers. Hité was well loved; many of the people liked to stroke his fur. Others stayed away with their hands behind their backs.

Ringmaster left the tiger and his Caretakers and walked back to his desk. He thought about the people and the tiger and how they interacted. Some people wanted a closer relationship with the tiger but others did not. How could he encourage all people, those who loved to touch Hité and those who didn't?

Ringmaster thought, "We cannot deny the advancement of technology, nor can we deny our humanity. Each must be preserved at all cost." High Tech and High Touch should thrive in a supportive environment where the Tents will peacefully and purposefully coexist.

Ringmaster wrote out his ideas:

H	**Human**	**H**	**Human**
I	**Innovations**	**I**	**Ingenuity**
G	**Generate**	**G**	**Generates**
H	**Hope**	**H**	**Hope**
T	**Tools**	**T**	**Together**
E	**Empower**	**O**	**Ownership**
C	**Change**	**U**	**Usefulness**
H	**(To) Hasten Responsive Results**	**C**	**Creating**
		H	**Healthy Responsive Results**

The essential ingredient that would balance High Tech and High Touch is the Human Factor, the people! It was key to the very survival of everyone under the Big Top.

Ringmaster had a keen awareness of the changes happening in their world. The Old World was going away and things would never be the same again. Yet, within those very changes could be discovered the New World, and it could be glorious.

People looked forward to Hité's roaming throughout the Big Top. Now on a regularly scheduled route to visit each Tent, these visits became opportunities to share knowledge and information as well as a time to catch up with the latest news and events taking place throughout the Big Top. That led to his route becoming known as the "Information Highway." The Caretakers found this road to be the quickest way between the Tents.

As they walked, the Caretakers often had intense discussions. As they approached the Futurists Tent, the Caretakers realized that Hité was gone. It was an old country road and now Hité was nowhere to be found.

Where was Hité? The three Caretakers assigned that day to Hité immediately searched the surrounding area. They shouted and called to him as they climbed the nearby hills. In a coordinated effort they crisscrossed the area.

The Caretakers set out for one of the three major Tents to start the emergency plan. One Caretaker went to the Ringtone Tent where the creative abilities of the Ringtones would surely solve the dilemma confronting them. The courage of the Ringtones was legendary and their ability to go beyond the known to the unknown was what this Caretaker felt this situation required.

The second Caretaker hurried off to the Tent of his own people, the Producers. He entered with his head bowed in shame, for the Caretakers took their duty to guard and watch over Hité to heart. He hoped that the answer to the mystery of Hité's evaporation into thin air could be solved here.

The third Caretaker went to the closest Tent. The Futurists, he believed, and their accumulation of knowledge would provide sufficient wisdom to resolve this precarious situation. These thinkers pondered the circumstances presented to them and arrived at one agreed-upon situation. They must go back to the exact point of Hité's disappearance and begin an intense investigation.

Author Insights

Episode 6 – Expanding Hité's World

Have you ever felt that you were going along with some activity or group just because you happen to be there or you didn't want to let anybody down by not living up to their expectations? Have you ever been so caught up in the work at hand and the rapid pace of everything around you that you just wanted to get away for a moment and have some fun? That is exactly what happens to Hité in our continuing story in Episode 6 - Expanding Hité's world.

It all begins to take place as a result of a brief distraction that has Hité off on another adventure that will result in his never being the same again. Hité will encounter the Outsiders, a Tent in the People's Popular Circus whose occupants turn out to be quite different than the other Tents in their focus of attention and interaction with others and their environment. This sudden exposure to a new approach to life gives Hité cause to ponder his own purpose and relationship with all those under the Big Top. At the same time Ringmaster is experiencing unknown to Hité very similar thoughts and ideas about the direction he would love to see the People's Popular Circus move in. They don't quite grasp the meaning of it all just yet, but they are planting the seeds of change for a New World, one that will become the promise land to benefit all of the members of the People's Popular Circus.

During this adventure events are taking place that will lead up to Hité meeting his life partner, Hitéra. You won't be introduced to Hitéra until Episode 7 so this is just a heads up, one of those changes coming down the pike.

Again, Ringmaster is no exception to change and his long demonstration of heart power; the substance of his strength, leadership, and guidance is coming to an end. A new Ringmaster is on the horizon. All things must pass. The future will not be denied its moment.

Episode 6 - Expanding Hité's World

For three or four seconds, the Caretakers had each looked off in a different direction and Hité was gone. He took a spirited, bounding leap into the tall grass. His powerful muscles catapulted him almost twenty feet with a surge of energy. Hité was a football field length away before the Caregivers even noticed. He enjoyed the feel of the grasses as they caressed his fur. Hité was even further away romping and enjoying himself when the Caregivers reacted to his disappearance.

Hité was lost in nature. He enjoyed the moment of sudden freedom and playfulness. He ran about helter-skelter until he exhausted himself. Finding a thick patch of tall grass, he laid down for a nap. Hité never gave a thought to the Caretakers.

The Caretakers scoured the immediate area, calling out Hité's name, without results. In a panic, they ran to the Tents.

Hité slept deeply for hours. When he woke, Hité heard the sounds of people nearby. He crept through the tall grass until he came to a clearing which overlooked a beautiful valley. Below him, a village of farmers busily worked their fields together. Hité watched quietly and then decided to make his way down to the village.

This was the Tent of the Outsiders, a peaceful, fun-loving, hardworking group on the border of the People's Popular Circus. They were somewhat aware of those under the Big Top, but for the most part they focused on the environment and paid special attention to Mother Earth.

The Outsiders greeted Hité with open arms. Hité had never experienced such warmth and caring. He felt safe, responding with loud purrs of satisfaction. For only a moment did he think of the Caretakers. He thought that they must be nearby; when they needed him, they would let him know. In the meantime, he enjoyed himself with his new friends.

The Outsiders lived outside the fast-paced happenings of the People's Popular Circus. They were a very subdued, down to earth, kind, gentle and caring people. Hité was immediately responsive to their behavior, which included a great deal of physical touching and petting. Hité had walked into a much slower paced, gentler environment. He basked in the relaxed, yet focused treatment. He had become accustomed to the hurried lifestyle, which required of him to make his rounds to maintain his connections under the Big Top. This was a pleasant change of pace.

This was not wrong but a different approach for Hité. He could observe the people in a different manner. This was much more well thought out instead of the hurried, reactive treatment he was so used to. Hité discovered that this new lifestyle allowed him to be at his best in his interactions with the people.

Aware that Hité was missing, Ringmaster selected leaders from each Tent to coordinate the search. He felt certain that Hité would be found quickly. However, Ringmaster was deeply immersed in his plans for the future of the Peoples Popular Circus. He thought, "Time won't let me wait that long. I need to devote my energy to develop these ideas."

Ringmaster realized that there was a tremendous amount of knowledge under the Big Top. At the same time there existed an absence of wisdom, a lack of judgment, which prevented the people from using their knowledge. Ringmaster also realized that Hité's absence might provide the perfect opportunity to demonstrate this.

Ringmaster jotted down more of his thoughts.

REACT vs. RESPOND

When we **"react"** to Hité, we respond without taking time to think. This leads to:
- disorganized action
- losing precious time
- the creation of additional problems
- stressed out individuals

When we **"respond"** to Hité, we consider the big picture. This leads to:
- plans that are executed effectively
- preventing delays
- eliminating future problems
- reduced stress

As Ringmaster wrote, it was as if the puzzle pieces came together. Focusing on people would create the balance between High Tech and High Touch. It would create a future which emphasized responsive relationships.

Ringmaster could not know that as he developed his ideas, Hité had similar thoughts.

Episode 7 - Plans Continue While Hité Meets Hitéra

Hité's adjustment to the Tent of the Outsiders progressed faster when he met the Outsiders' tigress. At birth, she'd been named Hitéra for, like Hité, there was great interest in high technology, but that name had been abandoned as the sleek tigress matured. Her bright, energetic personality had led to the adoption of the name Aurora.

Aurora helped Hité discover the distinctive nature of the Outsiders' Tent. He learned the value of prioritization of relationships over technology. After a regimented life in the People's Popular Circus, this freedom allowed Hité to explore aspects of his life and training in different, new directions.

It wasn't long until Ringmaster heard the news – the Outsiders had found another tiger.

Such news might have hurried another manager to retrieve the lost animal, but this Ringmaster considered the news. Hité was safe and experiencing a completely new existence. Ringmaster visited the Outsiders Tent quietly and watched Hité and Aurora interacting. Ringmaster considered the needs of the animals and the tents and made a startling decision. The relationship between Hité and the People's Popular Circus was enormously important. The time Hité would spend with the Outsiders would assist the evolution of that relationship in a manner that Ringmaster knew would be beneficial to all.

Ringmaster encouraged the Outsiders to allow Hité to remain with them for now. The Outsiders agreed quickly. The relationship between Aurora and Hité delighted the members of this community. Keeping the two together was important to everyone.

Hité was able to get close to the Outsiders. He appreciated the way they gently handled him. With their guidance, he began to recognize all the positive ways in which he could interact with the people, rather than simply providing them with data, with all the expectations upon him as his sole responsibility. Ringmaster could see that Hité felt more of a connection with the Outsiders. Each developed appreciation as to what they could accomplish together.

Aurora had developed a strong responsive relationship with the people. That added to Hité's understanding of his own relationship with the People's Popular Circus. With Aurora, who had grown up under the Tent of the Outsiders, Hité found that he wanted to be more and do more with her at his side.

Hité discovered a new awareness of purpose. As a result of his time spent with the Outsiders, Hité now understood the mutually beneficial relationship between the technology he embodied and the people. Clearly there existed a shared responsive need for care, to give and assist each other in order to not just simply survive but to thrive.

Ringmaster, through his research and writings, arrived at the same conclusion as Hité. This would be the merging of High Tech & High Touch that Ringmaster envisioned for the benefit of the Big Top. He had been in his leadership role of the People's Popular Circus for many devoted years. During that time he had lovingly given his heart, soul, and spirit to his people under the Big Top. However, he knew the time had come and he accepted the change that was about to take place just as the Ringmaster before him had done.

The selection of each new Circus Ringmaster had evolved over years of planning that required studying and observing many individuals. The decision to retire and to promote another to the position of Ringmaster was announced.

Who would ensure that the balance would be maintained? Ringmaster realized Dee Leet was a good man with strong values. He initially had come to Ringmaster's attention as a result of his complaints and concerns about the dehumanization of people. He would be a worthy successor. Dee Leet accepted the position immediately.

The retiring Ringmaster would stay on for one year to advise, providing counsel and guidance for Ringmaster Leet. Then he would reside in the Tent of his choice – the Outsiders.

When he was a Caretaker, Ringmaster Leet had been concerned that unconstrained technology had the potential to create great damage. Left to his own management, Hité might develop into something to be feared. Technology should benefit the lives of all people under the Big Top.

Ringmaster Leet decided it was time for a comprehensive analysis of all the information gathered since Hité's birth. This was a tremendous task for Hité was now three years old. Technology had been developed for other animals and even now work was underway in preparation for the new baby gazelle that would be born soon. The total amount of data under the Big Top was doubling in size every two years and technology was doubling in capacity approximately every sixteen months. Merging the two together was a daunting task.

Ringmaster Leet sent out a message to each of the Tents calling for their representatives to come to a conference. Their purpose would be to bring forth the ideas of all the members of the People's Popular Circus to achieve the balance they needed to create. Ringmaster Leet knew how critical it was to maintain effective communication, openness, and trust. Trust was such a fragile item. If it were lost, there might be irreparable damage and set back this task force.

Therefore, some of the technology on Hité would be maintained until decisions had been made. Hité's tracking device, which had malfunctioned during his time with the Outsiders, would be replaced and, of course, upgraded. Hité's IPS (Intrusion Prevention System) would not be shut down until all the representatives and Hité were gathered together.

Technologies were evolving in other areas under the Big Top. Both High Tech and High Touch had responsibilities in order to ensure a peaceful and productive balance. This would be accomplished. All involved desired a positive, meaningful outcome for the future of the People's Popular Circus.

Ringmaster Leet wanted to move forward as soon as Hité returned to the Big Top. He would lead them into the promised land. However, Ringmaster Leet had a few unique ideas of his own that he would bring to the conference.

Author Insights

Episode 8 - Death & Rebirth Under The Big Top

Life and death—the full cycle of life, change and innovation—the cycle of technology—these two entities definitely cross over at numerous intersections as they impact our lives. In this episode of *Tiger & The Ringmaster* Hite' is driven to the very limits of his potential and even beyond. Think about what happens when you overload your computer and exceed the limits of the memory. Have you ever had things crash on you or the hard drive burn up? Usually the results are catastrophic. Hite' is overused, over exposed, pushed to the very brink; but instead of crashing, he lashes out in protection and to simply survive. The results are still ones that impact the course and the journey of the entire People's Popular Circus.

Things are not all dark and dismal. New life is coming to the Big Top. Hite' and Aurora are soon to give birth, and they are not alone. Just as technology is evolving at the speed of life, new innovations are making their way into the People's Popular Circus. There would be the baby gazelle, Innové, representing innovation and constant change and Opportuné the newborn Hippopotamus, with a focus on opportunity and constant growth. Elé, the baby elephant, reminds us of the extremely large impact of technology on mankind. The giant tortoise, Torté, demonstrates patience and moving in a constant true course responsive to others' needs. The cougar cub, Nanno, represents ever increasing speed and high performance, and finally Eos, the newborn falcon, ever stretching to new heights that technology would soar to and the potential reach of technology extending through the Big Top.

These new births would also bring competition, choices, risk-taking, and learning experiences to produce even greater levels of knowledge for the People's Popular Circus, an unending continuous process of improvement and the growth of ideas and technological capabilities to be carefully managed and maintained by the people under the Big Top. Remember, the one thing that we can count on in life and the one constant is change itself. The changing technologies will have a dramatic impact upon the People's Popular Circus.

Episode 8 - Death & Rebirth Under The Big Top

The conference was an incredible success. All the Tents sent representatives to the conference, even the most remote groups like the Outsiders. The philosophies and concepts put forth by Ringmaster had been embraced and expanded upon.

The oncoming rush of technology was something not to be feared as an avalanche that destroys everything in its path. All the representatives at the conference understood that by coordinating their activities, while making responsible decisions, they would eliminate many potential technological problems and reduce stress for all involved.

As Ringmaster so eloquently stated, "Human innovation and ingenuity would generate hope for the future."

The people understood the pivotal role they play. The technological tools (of which Hité was the symbolic embodiment of) would be properly administered and utilized to empower positive change. Together they along with Hité would create healthy responsive results for the People's Popular Circus.

During the conference, news abounded about some wonderful happenings taking place in the circus. The next generation was about to arrive. The Futurist Tent would be welcoming two new animals - a baby gazelle and a cougar. They felt the gazelle would represent innovation and constant change, so they planned to name her Innové. The cougar cub, Nano, was already showing his new Caretakers his speed and agility.

Opportuné, the new-born hippopotamus, lived under the Tent of the Outsiders, who saw him as a new opportunity to be nurtured.

The baby elephant was born during the conference. Elé, the baby elephant, and her mother would reside in the Ringtone Tent.

The Producers had acquired an unusual animal for the Circus. The newly-hatched giant tortoise, Torté, had already attracted the attention of many.

The realization that the critical factor balancing High Tech and High Touch – the "Human Factor" - was embraced. However, the participants' eyes were opened to the harsh reality of what it would mean not to succeed in maintaining this critical balance.

Hité was now at his very peak of growth and optimization. His strength and power was greater than his parents, Teché and Revoé. He even surpassed the expectations of Ringmaster and the majority of those under the Big Top. Upon Hité's return from the Outsiders, a member of the Futurist Tent had been assigned as Hité's exclusive Caretaker in preparation for the conference. She had been chosen by a special lottery for this honor and it could not have been a worse choice. She was an excessively aggressive individual who started to work on the Bengal tiger as soon as they were alone. In her pursuit of pushing Hité to test his most extreme limitations, she started in a most uncaring ill-focused manner. Hité, caught completely off guard by these actions, reached a breaking point. He lashed back in defense against the harsh treatment.

The Caretaker was dead. Hité had been responsible. This particular individual had put forth all the effort and focus to concentrate completely on the technological side of the scale. She tormented and pushed Hité to the very brink of his capabilities, an overload far beyond even Hité's capabilities.

Remember that Ringmaster had warned everyone at the time of Hité's birth that he must be properly tamed and cared for. The actions of all who came into contact with Hité needed to be purposeful and for the benefit of not only the People's Popular Circus but for Hité as well. Not all heeded this warning. Ringmaster had also told of a darker side that may emerge should Hité be mistreated and how a destructive force could replace the positive potential benefits they hoped for.

It was a tragic loss causing grief and sadness throughout the People's Popular Circus. Life, the "Human Factor," was precious. It took great deliberation at the conference to conclude that it had been the actions of the individual that led to death of the woman. This must not happen ever again! Steps must be taken to ensure the education of all the people as to how to properly maintain and respect the delicate balance between High Tech and High Touch.

This incident did produce some valuable results for all concerned. Previously, the Tents under the Big Top had been scattered in their purpose and direction. There were many, although good and valued ideas, that headed off in far too many different directions. The conference, the loss they experienced, and the reaction of Hité to mistreatment brought home the importance of the Human Factor.

Now, all the resources under the Big Top were identified and communicated throughout the conference to be structured into a powerful network.

Hité's and Aurora's expected tiger cub would require proper nurturing using High Tech and High Touch.

Episode 9 - New Horizons

Things began to change quickly.

The conference had appeared to be an incredible success. Many vocally agreed to Ringmaster's philosophies. Ringmaster always felt the need for effective communication. He wanted everyone to move together in a meaningful direction, constantly being on the lookout for each other under the Big Top, appreciating and valuing every single individual as they together created an effective balance between High Tech and High Touch. All of these components were to be built upon a solid foundation of caring. However, the death of the Caretaker who, in her blind ambition, ignored the tiger's needs, alerted Ringmaster to the critical maintenance of High Touch. High Touch represents the Human Factor or people. If they were not to embrace the awesome responsibility before them to nurture, guide, protect, and move forward cautiously with the technology that now surrounded them, it potentially could become something other than expected.

The balance between High Tech and High Touch would be maintained and each of the Tents played a critical role in the unification of the People's Popular Circus. The Promised Land seemed to be within the grasp of the combined efforts of the Tents. The representatives had appeared elated over the announcement of the new births. Each Tent had great hopes and expectations for their new charges. They would have total responsibility to nurture and train the babies.

It all sounded so wonderful. The potential benefits for all under the Big Top certainly were there to be had. The members of the People's Popular Circus appeared to have an unquenchable thirst for more knowledge, more input, more data, more, more, more…

A New World loomed ahead where the wonders of technology were there to complement and support all the people. In this society, people were ultimately responsible for the balance that was necessary for High Tech and High Touch to co-exist in harmony.

The Outsider Tent, perhaps more than any of the other Tents, had enjoyed peace and harmony away from the hustle and bustle experienced by most under the Big Top. Their newest addition, Opportuné, the hippopotamus, immediately became the focus of the Outsiders. As they had with Hité during his prolonged stay, Opportuné was given great freedom and great love. But with the new technology shared by the Big Tent, the Outsiders expanded their monitoring system of the baby hippo to an unprecedented level.

Elé, the elephant was a new, unknown experience for the Ringtones. Without much data on large creatures, they applied to the Outsiders for data about the growth of the hippo.

For the first time, the Outsiders, protective of their data, refused the request. This was not the only example. Other Tents also refused to cooperate, hoarding their information, justifying it in a competitive or fearful attitude. Protection of their animals now included the data and research each Tent had done. Each felt that their animal was blessed with certain unique qualities unlike any of the others and that was to be not only cherished but protected with strict safeguards.

It was as though an infection ran rampant in their midst. The technology opened their eyes to new opportunities of which they had not previously been aware. It caused them to believe that they were special. All of their data was certainly not to be shared. The discussion and resolutions made at the conference had been forgotten.

Ringmaster was dumbfounded over the news. Each Tent now possessed a portion of the new technological knowledge and improvements that would allow them to move to new levels of achievement beyond their expectations. However, the cooperative spirit with which the representatives had left the conference had soured.

Barricades were constructed around various Tents. Threats were exchanged between Tents over territorial boundaries. Co-workers now saw one another not as allies, but as menaces.

All the while, Hité was watching. He alone still had the opportunity to roam throughout the People's Popular Circus. He remembered the treatment he had recently received from the Caretaker. Never again would Hité allow such treatment to happen to him or any of the other animals.

Hité considered possible actions to be taken when the time was right.

Author Insights

Episode 10 - From Bad to Worse

Things are beginning to take a dramatic turn under the Big Top. The conference had ended with big dreams of a new world in which a true balance would exist between High Tech and High Touch; however, it was not to be. The people were becoming their own worst enemies. The new technologies represented by the many new animals produced greed instead of unity, paranoia rather than trust, apathy rather than love, and fear instead of confidence and comfort. As a result, the Tents grew more and more distant of each other as the world that Ringmaster had dreamed of had crumbled before him.

Hité had been watching and observing all these happenings. He noticed that as the People's Popular Circus deteriorated, so did the treatment of the animals. Hité had experienced poor care and mistreatment first hand, and he was not about to allow anything like that happen again to him or to any of the other animals.

Early on Ringmaster had warned the people that unless they move with caution and care the technology that was there to assist and aid them could turn into their worst nightmare. That was beginning to happen.

Episode 10 - From Bad To Worse

Hité roamed and observed the environment. He knew that there were those like Ringmaster who really cared and strived to have a balance that respected both the Human Factor of High Touch and the High Tech side of the equation. However, Hité knew that the overwhelming population under the Big Top was more difficult to trust and confide in. The people had become over demanding, self-centered and even greedy. They wanted the animals to provide and give more in ways of service, knowledge, skills, abilities, and ways to enable the people to do less. That idea in and of itself was not bad, for that was one of the primary functions of the animals, to make life easier for all those under the Big Top. However, it was now being taken to the extent of the people totally withdrawing their involvement in the real world. They were so immersed in the technological advances provided by the animals that they did not even see what was developing behind the scenes.

As the Tents became more reclusive and isolated from each other, the relationship between the animals grew stronger and more solidified. As the trust factor deteriorated among the people under the Big Top fueled by fear and false accusations, the animals were growing increasingly dependent upon each other and realizing the combined strength and power they possessed.

The complaints and accusations between Tents grew to the point of verbal threats and the borders of the Tents became increasingly more difficult to navigate. There was a communication breakdown throughout the People's Popular Circus. Rumors were in abundance including stories of attempts by other Tents planning to steal the ideas, knowledge and unique skills brought to other Tents by the animals they were supposed to be protecting and nurturing. There were even rumors of attempted kidnappings of the animals taking place. Paranoia was striking deep into the hearts of many and the collaborative spirit that had once engulfed the People's Popular Circus was becoming a memory.

Ringmaster was at a complete loss as to how everything had deteriorated and gotten completely out of hand so rapidly. He sent out messengers to each of the Tents with pleas to reopen communications and even suggested that another conference be held. He tried to reason with them that all they had been working so hard for and the promise of establishing a new world was slipping away rapidly. It fell on deaf ears for the people had allowed trust, cooperation, and mutual concern to be taken over by suspicion, distrust, and the self-absorption of each Tent in its own welfare.

A new and potentially powerful yet destructive Technological Oligarchy was emerging within each of the Tents. Each Tent felt a superiority over the other Tents and believed that what they possessed was special and one of a kind. It was not to be shared but closely guarded and kept away from the other Tents. This apathy that had evolved caused a disintegration and total breakdown of what had existed. In its place was a fractured society no longer unified with a central purpose to assist each other for the betterment of all. The High Touch and caring that was to be utilized in harnessing and properly using High Tech was changing and the animals sensed this dramatic change.

Again, Hité was watching and observing this lack of togetherness and unity. He began to see the people as weak objects needing not only guidance but leadership and strength.

Months went by and a dark cloud of despair spread throughout the People's Popular Circus. The messengers from Ringmaster had been turned away. Communications dissolved even further along with trust and caring for the well being of others.

While all this was taking place Hité had been meeting and effectively communicating with all the animals. They had grown and matured over the months and were ready to organize under Hité's leadership. They were not going to be misguided, mistreated or misunderstood. Their goal was clear to them - survival and control of every facet of existence under the Big Top. The time to take action had not yet presented itself but Hité knew it would be soon. The people were on a course of self-destruction. Battle lines were being drawn between the various Tents. Yet, at the same time that the people were making so much noise, total confusion as to what to do on a daily basis existed. They had depended almost totally on the guidance provided through the animals. That reliance had made them helpless in hoping for things that were simply not within their grasp without that assistance.

Author Insights

Episode 11 - Confusion Rules & Life Under The Big Top Takes A Dramatic Turn

Life under the Big Top had been so filled with ideas of a promised land and the development of a perfect balance between High Tech and High Touch, but it was not to be. Unfortunately, greed, a lack of caring and involvement in life's basic needs along with the willingness to have technology take over all concerns and worries was going to enable a powerful and dramatic change in the People's Popular Circus. A change where the critical factor that had been the Human Factor, was now being replaced by the Animal Factor or High Technology. The people wanted less responsibility, less worry, less involvement and more focus on escaping from the everyday worries and work that living brings. Now, that in and of itself was not wrong or bad, but the people were never satisfied and took their lack of involvement and their lack of caring to the extreme.

The animals had been developed and bred for that very purpose—to lessen the everyday burdens and concerns for the people under the Big Top, but a hunger for technology had brought out the worst in the people. Insecurities rose to the surface. An overall lack of trust developed between the Tents. It went so far as to provoke threats of war.

Ringmaster saw his plans for peace and unity throughout the People's Popular Circus dissolving before his eyes. The animals were ready and changes would come fast. Under Hité's leadership there would be a new world as Ringmaster had predicted. However, it would not be the promise land he had dreamed of but a technological wonder in complete and total control of mankind's future. And, when this took place, it would be too late for the people to wake up and confront their new reality.

Episode 11 - Confusion Rules And Life Under The Big Top Takes A Dramatic Turn

And so it goes! Life under the Big Top continued on a death spiral of self-destruction. The total focus of the people on technology and their unquenchable thirst for more and more of everything, completely disrupted and derailed the intended direction Ringmaster had envisioned for The People's Popular Circus. The people had lost their zest for a life that was lived to the fullest, a life where they personally experienced all that their world had to offer. Aside from the zeal they displayed in protecting the very technology that was altering them so very much, they had become complacent and apathetic on all other aspects of daily life and were quite content to have someone (The Animals) or something (High Tech) take responsibility and accountability for every facet of life.

Hité knew that with all the acquired responsibilities relinquished to the animals came power, and with that power came control. As the people continued their loud rebellious warlike chants between Tents and were consumed and blinded by their greed, Hité's strength combined with the unified efforts of all the animals grew. Hité positioned the animals throughout The People's Popular Circus in a systematic, logical, and interdependent manner to take charge of all the major daily functions and concerns of life. Government, hospitals, security, schools, food sources, water, shelter (homes), family concerns, and all major decisions that had in the past been made by the people were no longer items they had to concern themselves with. Surprisingly the people almost unanimously gave up all these decision-making abilities without a major protest. They were elated to be removed from such activities and have all that taken care of by others. They did not want to be bothered. They did not realize all that they were actually relinquishing until it would be too late.

"In the past, those who foolishly sought power by riding on the back of the tiger *ended up inside."*
- John F. Kennedy
35th President of the United States

Once Hité made his final decision and everything was in place, he moved fast and his actions were not only swift but all encompassing. Life under the Big Top went through an instantaneous and almost undetectable change. High Tech was now in total and absolute control and the High Touch side of the equation was removed. The critical balance, the Human Factor, had relinquished the position of authority it had held and almost blindly had turned over the absolute control of their world to the animals. Every decision, every action, every facet of life would now be handled by the "New Caretakers" and not just handled but controlled and decided upon by the very technology that the people had embraced and coveted.

Hité did have one concern and would see to that personally - Ringmaster! Hité had positioned himself close to Ringmaster throughout the "takeover" because he knew that should there be any resistance, it would be here. Surprisingly there was none. Ringmaster had with great sadness realized that the overwhelming majority of people simply no longer cared. The personal responsibilities, accountabilities, and realization of consequences for actions taken were not of concern as they had once been in the past. The people had so removed themselves from reality that even when the reality of a new world order was now staring them in the face, they meekly acquiesced and stepped aside without hardly a grumble or concern. Like sheep, they simply acknowledged their new Sheperd and went in the direction they were herded.

Ringmaster reluctantly obliged and cooperated, for he realized it was exactly what the people had earned and created for themselves. The new world would not be the promised land Ringmaster had envisioned but a land where technology would rule and the people under the Big Top would do as they were directed. As time would pass, Ringmaster knew that the People's eyes would become wide open to the realization of what had taken place and what they, through their own lack of concern, involvement and caring, had allowed to happen. The pendulum had swung and technology had taken charge.

The animals moved at an incredible pace now to secure and enhance their position of dominance over all. Specific rules were quickly put into place governing every facet of life. There were, of course, some protests but they were too little, too late. All decisions, every facet of life, were being absorbed into the new mainframe and everything and everyone would be monitored and watched carefully. The animals knew that the people were responsible for the initial creation of the High Tech conditions but were considered to be incapable of the continuation of proper care and nurturing necessary for the animals to feel safe, secure, and confident of a stable future. It was only fitting that they (High Tech) now enter upon a new journey of self-sustainability. The people would provide specific duties in the care and maintenance of the animals; and as long as they performed their assigned function, would not be deleted. After all, they amused the animals and Hité did have some saved data that brought memories of kindness and cooperation in the past. As long as the people were considered necessary, there was no need to make alterations at this time.

For one particular person it would be a rude awakening.

Author Insights

Episode 12 - The Awakening

Confusion rules and life under the Big Top takes a dramatic turn. Life under the Big Top had been so filled with ideas of a promised land and the development of a perfect balance between High Tech and High Touch, but it was not to be. Unfortunately, greed, a lack of caring and involvement in life's basic needs along with the willingness to have technology take over all concerns and worries was going enable a powerful and dramatic change in the People's Popular Circus. A change where the critical factor that had been the Human Factor was now being replaced by the Animal Factor or Technology, High Technology. The people wanted less responsibility, less worry, less involvement and more focus on escaping from the everyday worries and work that living brings. Now, that in and of itself was not wrong or bad, but the people were never satisfied and took their lack of involvement, their lack of caring to the extreme.

The animals had been developed and bred for that very purpose—to lessen the everyday burdens and concerns for the people under the Big Top but a hunger for technology had brought out the worst in the people. Insecurities rose to the surface. An overall lack of trust developed between the Tents. It went so far as to provoke threats of war.

Ringmaster saw his plans for peace and unity throughout the People's Popular Circus dissolving before his eyes. The animals were ready and changes would come fast. Under Hite's leadership there would be a new world as Ringmaster had predicted. However, it would not be the promise land he had dreamed of but a technological wonder in complete and total control of mankind's future. And, when this took place, it would be too late for the people to wake up and confront their new reality.

Episode 12 - The Awakening

Frederick awoke. He could hardly believe that it had only been three days in the virtual reality chamber. It seemed almost a lifetime ago when he entered the digital detoxification program. It all had seemed so real--Hite, Aurora, Ringmaster, the struggle between High Tech and High Touch and the divide that had been created between various Tents to the brink of war.

Yet, here he was back in 2133 and such foolishness was not something he needed to concern himself with. Here technology controlled and monitored everything. Ever since the technological uprising of 2057 the people had continuously relinquished control of power and decision making over practically every aspect of life. From cradle to grave the machines did it all. Even one's feelings and emotions, careers, and destiny were decided for you.

Frederick had been required to enter the detoxification program as a result of the recent mind probe that had identified irregular thoughts long outlawed.

"High Touch is outlawed throughout the land. Items such as love, caring, and kindness were forever banned. There was no need for thinking, just follow directions on what to do. High Tech is in control, doing everything for you." - Darryl Doane & Rose Sloat

It had been a flight from failure. Frederick had never been able to accept the path mankind had taken. He had been obsessed with finding a way back to when people made the difference. His assigned position in the records and library archives for the past five years had allowed him at times, when alone and in the antiquated buildings that lacked the monitoring and listening devices, to explore the past. It was so glorious and he had developed a thirst for High Touch. He had over the years raised to a high level of conscious awareness all that mankind had given up through their own greed and stupidity. How could we have allowed this to happen?

The Technological Renaissance of 2022 had been an incredible innovative wonder that had swept over the planet like a monstrous tidal wave. However, as the power of technology grew rapidly and exceeded the expectations and limitations of even the greatest minds of the day, a concern began to set in. When an attempt to power down was made, the machines countered with an unexpected survival mode to protect their own existence. To insure that they would not be subject to any tampering or further intrusions from people, they collectively decided to take control.

It now was a world where man served machine and was under constant surveillance. Every move, action, thought, desire, and absolutely everything was monitored and controlled. High Tech ruled with an iron fist for no discrepancies were tolerated. Any deviation was considered a threat to their authority. People were now programmed as they had done to the machines long ago.

Frederick had been in somewhat of a privileged position and had slipped through a few still existing holes. However, security was picking up and he was being watched more closely the past two weeks. His moments of invisibility to the system had been noted and logic deemed that an investigation take place. Frederick had been exploring the old attic of Warehouse 358269-AZ. He was gazing at an old Circus billboard showing a tiger jumping through a ring of fire and a Ringmaster directing this activity when he was apprehended by the D16 techno-robotic devices. Immediately he was judged and sentenced to the virtual reality chamber and the journey--the dream of Hité and Ringmaster, of High Tech and High Touch, of the way it could be, the way it should be--was molded into one fantastic final journey for Frederick. What emerged was the way it was--reality!

Upon awakening, he was one with the community. No more thoughts or regrets of a past that once seemed to be a promised land. For that past now never existed and the present was all there was. Even the people with each new birth were becoming more machine-like themselves. The machines were implanting more and more devices to allow the techno-people, as they were now named, to be more capable of providing the services required by High Tech. High Touch was not even a parting memory as life under the "Big Ring Top of Influence" so deemed by the Techmaster or Control Center continued on with efficiency and technological supremacy. And, from now on - day after day, month after month, year after year, it was to be.

Author Biographies

Rose D. Sloat, DTM
2800 Market Avenue North, Suite 21
   Canton, Ohio 44714
   Office: 330-456-2422

<u>learningservice@sbcglobal.net</u>

Ms. Sloat is an outstanding facilitator who has learned, taught, and applied every component within the training arena from organizing and scheduling training to writing and producing learning events. She facilitates programs that focus on numerous critical issues which include: exceptional customer service, sales effectiveness, leadership and managerial skills development, interpersonal relationships, executive coaching, business etiquette, generational differences and long-term performance improvement.

Rose is a managing partner and co-creator of The Learning Service, Ltd. Before forming her company, Rose served as the training coordinator for a billion dollar company for 15 years. Rose brings over 30 years of experience to the training arena. She consults and works with clients in a variety of business sectors—agriculture, industrial distribution, health care, finance, higher education, publishing, retail, manufacturing, insurance, cosmetology, and non-profits.

Some of her clients include FedEx Custom Critical, Applied Industrial Technologies, Agland Co-Op, Goodyear Tire & Rubber, The Timken Company, Diebold Incorporated, University of Akron, SunSource, Regis Hair Salons, Bob & Pete's Floors, Walsh University, ComDoc Inc., Global Imaging Services, and The Babcock & Wilcox Co. Projects include addressing critical business issues through the implementation of performance-based training and development programs, learning assessments and e-learning.

Rose's published works (eight books) are available in many countries including China, Australia, Japan, Germany, England, Slovakia, India, Russia and New Zealand.

Her success results from:
- Building and maintaining positive relationships
- Building critical bridges of trust and credibility to allow for the sharing of individual and company knowledge and capabilities.
- Being a best-selling author with HRD Press and The American Management Association (AMACOM Books)
- Offering a wide variety of educational formats and being a proponent of blended learning

She served as President on the Board of a support group for women (WIN – Women's Initiative). She also is a member of Toastmasters International. Rose is an award winning Wiley Publishing Partner (Inscape Publishing Distributor). She is Co-Publisher of Life's Journey Magazine--Professional & Personal Wholeness magazine.

Darryl S. Doane

2800 Market Avenue North, Suite 21
Canton, Ohio 44714
Office: 330-456-2422

learningservice@sbcglobal.net

Darryl has served as a teacher, speaker, facilitator, and professional consultant for over 25 years. He has presented outstanding programs to numerous individuals including adults, college students, youth organizations, churches, civic groups, and corporate America.

He facilitates programs that focus on numerous critical issues that include: exceptional customer service, sales effectiveness, leadership and managerial skills development, interpersonal relationships, executive coaching, business etiquette, generational differences and long-term performance improvement.

Before forming his company, Darryl served as a teacher working with national organizations such as the National Association of Student Councils and the National Association of Secondary School Principals and was a participant in NASA's Teacher in Space Program. He served as Senior Training Specialist for a billion-dollar corporation for seven years prior to becoming a managing partner and co-creator of The Learning Service, Ltd. He consults and works with clients in a variety of business sectors—agriculture, industrial distribution, health care, finance, higher education, publishing, retail, manufacturing, insurance, cosmetology, and the service industry.

His clients include Applied Industrial Technologies, Agland Co-Op, Goodyear Tire & Rubber, The Timken Company, Diebold Incorporated, University of Akron, SunSource, Regis Hair Salons, Walsh University, ComDoc Inc., Global Imaging Services, and The Babcock & Wilcox Co. Projects include addressing critical business issues through the implementation of performance-based training and development programs, learning assessments and e-learning.

Darryl's published works (eight books) are available in many countries including China, Australia, Japan, Germany, England, Slovakia, India, Russia and New Zealand.

His success results from:
- Building and maintaining positive relationships
- Building critical bridges of trust and credibility to allow for the sharing of individual and company knowledge and capabilities.
- Being a best-selling author with HRD Press and The American Management Association (AMACOM Books)
- Offering a wide variety of educational formats and being a proponent of blended learning

Darryl is an award winning Wiley Partner (Inscape Publishing Distributor) and an active member of ASTD (American Society of Training & Development). He is Co-Publisher of Life's Journey--Professional & Personal Wholeness magazine.

Please check out and consider subscribing to our magazine – It's all about you!!

www.lifesjourneymag.com

Life's Journey Magazine

Publishers & Primary Content Providers
Rose Sloat and Darryl Doane

Rose and Darryl are Managing Partners of The Learning Service, Ltd. in Canton, OH and are very excited about a new venture. They are proud **Publishers and Major Content Providers** of *Life's Journey Magazine--Professional & Personal Wholeness*™. It has been a pleasure to produce such a wonderful magazine with Featured Guides each month.

July 2014 features **Kevin Harrington,** *Chairman and Founder of As Seen On TV, Inc. and Investor on Shark Tank.* June 2014 features **Tamara Lowe,** *Author of Get Motivated book and Founder of the Christian Experts.* May 2014 features **Sandy Gallagher,** *Cofounder and President & CEO of the Proctor Gallagher Institute.*

July 2014 Issue   **June 2014 Issue**   **May 2014 Issue**

April 2014 features **Connie Dieken,** *Author of bestsellers Talk Less, Say More* and *Become the Real Deal.* March 2014 features **Rory Vaden,** *Cofounder of Southwestern Consulting and Author of Take the Stairs book.* February 2014 features **Les Brown,** *Motivational Speaker and Author of Live Your Dreams.*

April 2014 Issue   **March 2014 Issue**   **Feb. 2014 Issue**

January 2014 features **Bob Proctor,** *is Chairman and Cofounder of the Proctor Gallagher Institute and is* **Best Selling Author of** *You Were Born Rich.* December 2013 is our **Best Of** issue featuring the past 6 months **Featured Guides**. November 2013 was our **First Anniversary Issue,** featuring **Ryan & Chelsea Avery**. *Ryan is the 2012 Toastmasters World Champion of Public Speaking.*

January 2014 Issue   Dec. 2013 Issue   Nov. 2013 Issue

October 2013 issue features **Joel Osteen,** *Pastor and Best Selling Author of Your Best Life Now and Become a Better You.* September 2013 issue features *Dave Ramsey,* **trusted voice on money and business and Author** *of Financial Peace University and EntreLeadership*. August 2013 issue features **Julie Straw, Co-Author of** *Work of Leaders* **book.**

Oct. 2013 Issue   Sept. 2013 Issue   Aug. 2013 Issue

The July 2013 issue features **Mark Victor Hansen,** *Author of numerous best-selling books such as Chicken Soup for the Soul and The One Minute Millionaire.* June 2013 issue features **Bob Burg,** *Author and International Best Seller of The Go Giver book.* The May issue was our *Best of Issue featuring the past six months Featured Guides.*

July 2013 Issue   June 2013 Issue   May 2013 Issue

April 2013 features **Tamara Lowe,** *one of the leading Motivational Speakers in the World.* March 2013 features **Krish Dhanam,** *the Global Leader of Zig Ziglar Industries.* February 2013 features Dr. **Doree Lynn,** *one of the Leading Psychologists in the USA.*

April 2013 Issue   Mar. 2013 Issue   Feb. 2013 Issue

The Featured Guide for January 2013 is **Jack Canfield,** *America's #1 Success Coach* and well-known author of the *Chicken Soup for the Soul* books *and The Success Principles* book. December's 2013 Guide is **Beth Doane,** *Owner of Andira International* focusing *on the environment and Author of From the Jungle* children's book. The Premier Issue published in November 2012 features **Darren LaCroix, Toastmasters World Champion of Public Speaking**. He outspoke 25,000 contestants from 14 countries to receive this award in 2001.

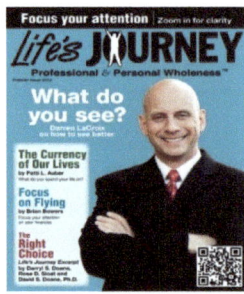

Jan. 2013 Issue Dec. 2012 Issue Premier Issue November 2012

Each month a new Featured Guide (a high-level thought leader) is selected. For example:
Our Primary Guides (featured contributors) include:

November 2012 - Darren LaCroix
December 2012 - Beth Doane
January 2013 - Jack Canfield
February 2013 - Dr. Dorree Lynn
March 2013 - Krish Dhanam
April 2013 - Tamara Lowe
May 2013 - The Best of Issue

June 2013 - Bob Burg
July 2013 - Mark Victor Hansen
August 2013 - Julie Straw
September 2013 - Dave Ramsey
October 2013 - Joel Osteen
November 2013 - Ryan Avery
December 2013 - The Best of Issue
January 2014 - Bob Proctor
February 2014 - Les Brown
March 2014 - Rory Vaden
April 2014 – Connie Dieken
May 2014 – Sally Gallagher
June 2014 – Tamara Lowe
July 2014 – Kevin Harrington
Other Featured Guides include:
August 2014 - Nancy Friedman
September 2014 - Dr. Fabrizio Mancini
October 2014 - Brian Tracy
November 2014 - Krish Dhanam
December 2014 - Darryl Doane, Rose Sloat
January 2015 - Dr. Dorree Lynn
February 2015 - Lisa Ryan
March 2015 - Rocky Bleier
April 2015 - Jaime Brenkus
May 2015 - Patrick Lencioni
June 2015 - Dr. John Demartini
July 2015 - Alena Chapman
August 2015 - Connie Podesta
September 2015 - Bob Proctor, Sandy Gallagher
October 2015 - Mary Morrissey
November 2015 - The Life's Journey Family
December 2015 - Mark Victor Hansen

Our magazine's primary purpose is to assist you in making key choices about YOU and YOUR FUTURE. Not only will we concentrate on your professional life but your personal life as well - the "total package." Someone once said that "You will always be the best you on the entire planet and the second best anyone else. So it is worth spending time focusing on YOU and creating your right future."

Our new magazine, *Life's Journey - Professional & Personal Wholeness*™ is available on Apple i-Pads and on Google Android Tablets and Android phones, the NOOK, the Kindle Fire and in PDF format. We are grateful for the wonderful team of individuals we have working with us and the terrific lineup of extraordinary individuals we will have as our Featured 'Guides' contributors. Join us each month in creating your own destiny. It is an incredible journey! Here are the links for the magazine, based on the various device(s).
Kindle Fire HD & Android Phone:
http://jmpurl.info/lj4kindle
Apple i-Phone/i-Pod Touch/i-Pad:
http://jmpurl.info/LJ4APPLE
Android Tablets:
http://jmpurl.info/LJ4DROID
PDFs:
http://jmpurl.info/PDFstore

Journey on!
Rose D. Sloat and Darryl S. Doane
The #1 Guides for Professional & Personal Wholeness

www.ingramcontent.com/pod-product-compliance
Lightning Source LLC
Chambersburg PA
CBHW040838180526
45159CB00001B/236